Military UFO Encounters

True Cases of Military Alien Encounters

Conrad Bauer

Copyrights

Disclaimer and Terms of Use

ISBN: 9781081867126

Printed in the United States

Contents

What Does Uncle Sam Know?

Second only to the debate about whether or not UFOs and aliens actually *exist* are the questions about what the government does and does not know about them and the potential threat that such entities may pose to our planet. But when we speak of the government, who are we talking about, exactly? The lawmakers? The elected officials? The bureaucrat appointees of the deep state? Or are we talking about those in charge of our armed forces?

Because no matter how liberal a democracy may be, when push comes to shove, it is always the military top brass that has the real power. It is the military, after all, that defends a nation's borders to maintain that nation as a sovereign entity.

President Dwight D. Eisenhower coined the term "military-industrial complex" to describe the power that military might holds over modern society. In his farewell address to the American public, Eisenhower warned of the dangers posed by this institution and described his fears that it could very well spin out of civil control. Coincidentally enough, Eisenhower has since become a darling of conspiracy theorists who claim that he was privy to the very first open contact between the U.S. government/military and visitors from another world.

So while we often ask what our *government* knows about UFOs and extraterrestrials, perhaps we should be asking what the *military* knows. Unlike elected officials, the military top brass is not given to slips of the tongue. They are experts at keeping things on a need-to-know basis. Could it be that the people the Pentagon are aware of exactly what is going on in our skies—but don't think the rest of us need to know? Keep reading this book as we explore all of the possibilities.

huge and had a ring of "undulating orange lights" rapidly blinking all along its edges.

As airplanes were still in their infancy, featuring wooden propellers and canvas-covered fuselages, there was not much chance that this was an enemy aircraft. The behemoth most closely resembled a Zeppelin, but no Zeppelin was shaped like a round saucer, and none would have had a ring of flashing lights—strobe lights hadn't been invented back in 1917. So this saucer-shaped apparition was clearly of an entirely different order than anything standard aviation technology could produce. The best theory that Waitzrik and Richthofen could come up with was that it was some sort of prototype developed by the Americans, who had just recently entered the war. It was only many years later, after the UFO phenomenon went mainstream, that Peter Waitzrik began to believe that they had encountered something completely out of this world.

In the heat of the moment, though, the Red Baron wasted no time in engaging what he assumed was a new type of enemy aircraft. He got the saucer in his sights and immediately let loose with his machine guns. To the Germans' astonishment, the bullets ripped through the vehicle and in Waitzrik's words it "dropped like a rock" and crashed into the woods below, "sheering off tree limbs" as it went. Waitzrik and Richthofen then watched as "two little baldheaded guys" pulled themselves out of the wreckage and wandered off into the trees.

The Red Baron died in combat (against terrestrial opponents) the following year, but Waitzrik had the rest of the 20th century to mull over what he had seen. The more he thought about it, the stranger it seemed, and by the last years of his life, as a centenarian in the late 1990s, he had become convinced that what Richthofen shot down that day was not an experimental American aircraft—in fact, it wasn't an aircraft from *any* earthly

4

If a group such as the Brookings Institution, for example, wanted to argue that the public should not be informed about the presence of ET visitors, from then on and until all eternity, all they had to do was point to the panic caused by this one solitary broadcast. But was the Pentagon really behind this radio program? Was it really a giant PSYOP conducted to gather information or prove a point? Where's the proof of *that*?

Well, actually, there is plenty of evidence for just such a thing. This could be the worst-kept secret of any clandestine program ever. Perhaps due to widespread embarrassment at having fallen for the fake news, no one at the time bothered to look very deeply into the true origins of the Orson Welles production. But if one simply follows the money trail, Welles was funded by the Rockefeller Foundation, a wealthy group very much involved with government projects. Add to this the fact that the infamous Council on Foreign Relations had partnered with the Rockefeller Foundation to orchestrate every detail of the production, and you already have a compelling case for conspiracy. One of Welles' handlers was the esteemed psychologist Dr. Paul F. Lazarfield. Now, why would a psychologist be involved with a radio drama if not to help gauge the psychological reaction of the public? It is also said that CBS employees Frank Stanton and Dr. Hadley Cantril commissioned Welles to do the broadcast with the stated intent of analyzing the "behavior of citizens" who listened to the programming.

Now, the mere mention of the Rockefellers and the Council on Foreign Relations is probably enough to convince the conspiracy buffs, but what about the rest of us? Couldn't it all have been a coincidence? The interesting thing is, while the initial intentions of CBS, the Rockefellers, and the Council on Foreign Relations are not explicitly documented, their actions afterward are clear. Even if it wasn't their explicit goal to study the reaction of a panicked population terrified at the thought of alien invasion, that's exactly what they did after the broadcast. Dr. Cantril's associates quickly slapped together a study quantifying every detail of the public's reaction. One can only imagine that military analysts did the exact same thing.

So whether it was on purpose or by fortuitous accident, the Orson Welles broadcast proved to be a perfect experiment on how the public would react to an announcement of ET contact— and the prognosis was not good. You can rest assured that the military took note of every detail and compiled, compartmentalized, and stored away these findings for future reference.

Alleged UFO Recovery by Nazi Germany

The previous chapter explored possible U.S. maneuvering to gauge public reaction to ETs in the 1930s. As surprising as this may be, it is completely dwarfed by what some allege the German government was up to during this same decade.

Adolf Hitler came to power in 1933, and the conspiracy theorists say that shortly afterward he and his fellow Nazis came into contact with visitors from another world. The Nazi Party had always been interested in communing with extra-human intelligence, and as soon as they were running the show in Germany they began sending expeditions to the ends of the Earth in search of it. Most famously, teams of Nazi scientists were sent to remote places such as the Himalayas and Antarctica in search of this supposed secret knowledge. But according to UFO enthusiasts, the Nazis didn't have to travel to find their otherworldly contacts, because an otherworldly contact found them first.

In this narrative, the first major UFO crash was not in Roswell in 1947—it was in Nazi Germany in 1936 when an extraterrestrial vehicle came down in the remote reaches of the Black Forest. As in the Roswell account, this UFO is said to have been caught in an electrical storm which short-circuited its navigational system.

German troops were alerted to the crash and quickly converged on the scene. They observed a huge circular ship—a formerly flying saucer—half submerged in a mound of dirt and obliterated trees. Watching from a distance, they saw extraterrestrial beings emerge from the craft. They were short, with disproportionately long arms and oversized heads. Their skin had a greyish cast (enter the infamous "grey aliens" of UFO lore) and they were dressed in some sort of black jumpsuits. They all had black boxes attached to their belts, and these boxes seemed to project some sort of energy field around them.

German scientists would later ascertain that this energy field was actually a projected "spacesuit" that created a self-contained personal atmosphere around each being, keeping the air pressure and oxygen levels comfortable for them no matter where they were. But these atmospheric bubbles did not stop bullets, a fact which was ascertained on the spot when three of the beings approached the watching Nazis and were promptly massacred by machine-gun fire. So much for first contact; the men of the Wehrmacht were apparently just as quick on the trigger as their military forebear Manfred von Richthofen.

The more circumspect Nazi high command, however, realized the potential value of the technology housed within the strange craft and had it hauled off to the remote but massive Wewelsburg castle, which was being used as a headquarters of the Nazi SS. Here, scientists worked assiduously to reverse engineer as much of the technology as possible—a feat something akin to a 19th-century locomotive engineer trying to come to grips with a stealth bomber. Nevertheless, the Nazis were known for their feverish, frenetic pace when it came to military projects, and apparently they were able to glean some information from the extraterrestrial craft that led to breakthroughs in their own propulsion systems. Within a few years, they would surprise the world with both the first jet fighters and the first forms of advanced rocketry.

Not only that, some allege that the crashed UFO led to experiments with anti-gravity craft that had the potential to bend space and even time itself. The strangest fruit of the alleged Nazi program to reverse engineer the UFO recovered from the Black Forest was a device called *Die Glocke*, which is German for "the Bell". This bell or acorn-shaped object was supposedly the Nazis' most highly classified piece of technology. Although no one seems certain if it was a vehicle, a weapon, or some combination of both, it is described as being 15 feet tall and 8 feet wide. The incredibly strong metal alloys of *Die Glocke* were able to withstand powerful electromagnetic and gravitational forces generated from "two counter-rotating cylinders" located just below the underside of the contraption and powered by a mystery element called "Xerum 525".

The intense energy field around the object created a deadly working environment for the scientists tasked with unraveling its mysteries. Some dropped dead after their "blood congeal[ed] within their veins" into a greasy goo as they were running tests on *Die Glocke*. The device also had a pesky habit of trying to shoot off into the air, so it was chained down to a steel ring strangely reminiscent of Stonehenge.

This steel ring, at least, has been verified to exist and can be viewed near the Czech border to this very day. Of course, the mere existence of a steel ring doesn't exactly prove that the venue was a test site for UFO technology reverse engineered by the Nazi military. The official story is that the ring was part of a water cooling tower, which seems reasonable enough— although, as any good conspiracy theorist knows, a good cover story is sometimes too good to be true.

But even if *Die Glocke* existed, and the steel rings were part of the launch pad from which this tremendous power source was activated, what was the purpose of it all? If the Nazis had an anti-gravity device, why didn't they use it in the war along with their jets and rocket planes?

Some think that the answer is that their tests of the device were a little too successful, achieving nothing short of ripping a hole in the very fabric of space and time and propelling Die Glocke from 1940s Germany to 1960s America. Because it was during that decade that a mysterious craft was seen streaking across the skies of the U.S., only to crash-land in Kecksburg, Pennsylvania—and as we will discuss later in this book, many conspiracy theorists believe that the Kecksburg UFO was actually the object that the Germans called *Die Glocke*.

So, what's the verdict? Were Hitler's vaunted wonder weapons the result of reverse engineered alien tech from a crashed UFO? The truth may very well be out there, but it's completely entangled in web after web of conspiracy theory.

The Foo Fighters of World War II

Nowadays, the Foo Fighters are a band with former Nirvana drummer Dave Grohl at the helm. But back in World War II, "foo fighters" was the term used by military pilots to describe UFOs.

One of the first of these sightings occurred towards the end of 1941, when British pilots began to report anomalous aerial objects that would chase or fly alongside their aircraft. Although these objects did not attack them, they did seem to interfere with the navigational and electrical components of the RAF fighter planes—a dangerous and potentially deadly phenomenon for the befuddled pilots.

Another strange foo fighter sighting in September of 1941 occurred at sea aboard the SS *Pułaski*, a Polish vessel chartered by the British military. Allied troops aboard this ship bore witness to a "strange globe glowing with green light" that hovered above them.

The British eventually became so concerned about such sightings that in 1943 they created what could be termed the first UFO study group. Countless reports of encounters with foo fighters were analyzed by some of the best minds the United Kingdom could provide.

The Americans got their turn with the foo fighters in late 1944, shortly after the successful invasion of Nazi-occupied Europe known as D-Day. As U.S. troops poised on the French/German border ready to deliver their knockout blow to the Nazis, American pilots in the skies above them began to notice some strange activity in German airspace. One report from late November, for example, details an incident in which a Bristol Beaufighter crew saw "eight to 10 bright orange lights off the left wing—flying through the air at high speed." These strange luminous globes positioned themselves at the plane's wingtips and then kept pace in perfect synchronicity. Many other pilots reported similar sightings—but strangely enough, their radar usually reported nothing at all.

Yet more and more of the inexplicable foo fighters were harassing Allied pilots. They never took any overtly hostile actions—the biggest problem continued to be that they occasionally caused electrical failures in the planes they approached—but at first their mere presence was usually enough to spook even the most seasoned of pilots. As the Allies began to encounter German jets and rockets, though, they came to conclude that the foo fighters were just one more Nazi wonder weapon.

After the war ended, however, it was realized that as advanced as some German weapons programs were, they could not account for these strange craft. Some began to speculate that the foo fighter sightings were military encounters of the extraterrestrial kind. Nearly a decade later, the U.S. military attempted to seriously address what some of its pilots had witnessed during the war. Under the auspices of the UFO study group Project Blue Book, an ad hoc think tank known as the

Robertson Panel was commissioned to finally get to the bottom of things.

The panel headed by scientist Howard P. Robertson found a convenient, plausible explanation for the majority of foo fighter cases in the phenomenon known as Saint Elmo's fire. Known to seagoing vessels for centuries, Saint Elmo's fire is a rather spooky but completely natural phenomenon in which luminous plasma is produced when air brushes against a sharp or pointed object—such as the wingtips of an airplane. Conspiracy theories about government cover-ups aside, for the many foo fighter sightings in which pilots reported balls of light traveling along the edge of their wings, this explanation actually makes a lot of sense.

But try as the Robertson Panel might to debunk all the foo fighter claims, it found a small percentage of truly unexplainable reports that continue to defy all explanation to this day.

The Battle of Los Angeles

One of the strangest and best documented military encounters with a UFO occurred on February 24, 1942. The U.S. had recently entered World War II on the heels of the bombing of Pearl Harbor by Imperial Japan, and Americans—most especially on the West Coast—were in a state of extreme anxiety.

For this reason, both the alleged UFO sighting over California and the frantic attempts of the U.S. military to shoot the UFO down are often laughed off as nothing more than wartime jitters. The incident is usually considered a classic case of mass hysteria that got the best of civilians and military personnel alike. On the surface, that seems like a reasonable enough explanation. But as readily as many have accepted it, a further examination of what actually happened seems to rip that theory to shreds. Because the fact is that something really *was* in the air that night—and it wasn't just wartime anxiety.

A giant unidentified object was spotted hovering over the California coastline. The craft was witnessed by hundreds if not thousands of people, lit up by search lights, and even photographed. Some calmer souls among the observers may have shrugged and dismissed the wingless object sailing through the skies as nothing more than a blimp or some sort of reconnaissance balloon. But what happened next proved that it was nothing of the sort.

Soon after the craft appeared, the air-raid sirens began to go off and a total blackout of several city blocks was issued so that antiaircraft gunners could get a better view of the interloper. This was not a drill; this was not a joke. Even the military observers on the ground truly believed that U.S. airspace had been invaded by the enemy. With the blackout in effect, the object was lit up like a Christmas tree by search lights and ground-based gun batteries began to unload on it.

Now, if you recall the account of the Red Baron blasting a UFO from the skies with a pair of light machine guns, you might be justified in assuming that this sustained barrage of cannon fire made short work of the object hovering over Los Angeles. Well, maybe the Baron caught *his* ETs with their pants (or force fields) down, or maybe the aliens had learned their lesson from that earlier incident and were taking no such chances this time around—because round after round slammed into the craft with absolutely no effect whatsoever.

Under the glare of the searchlights, stunned onlookers watched as anti-aircraft shells bounced off the glowing object. (The fact that shrapnel from shells could be seen ricocheting off the craft also counters the claim that witnesses had confused the moon with an alien craft, since obviously anti-aircraft rounds would not have been able to reach the lunar surface!) The guns continued pummeling this object as it listlessly drifted across the skies all the way up to 4:15 AM the next morning. They stopped not because the UFO was shot down at that point, but because that was when it decided to peacefully depart the scene.

As the smoke cleared, it became obvious that all the incessant firing of the anti-aircraft guns had done was rain destruction down upon Los Angeles. There was widespread damage from the falling shrapnel. A number of civilians had been injured and a few even killed by the ammunition that had bounced back to the ground from the impervious UFO above. In a newspaper account the next day, the event was summed up as "Surreal—[with the UFO] hanging, [like a] magic lantern. It was like the Fourth of July but so much louder. The military was shooting like crazy on it, but they couldn't deal any damage."

If the so-called "Battle of Los Angeles" against this one unknown craft went so badly, I would really hate to see what an actual war of the worlds would look like! But just what were the military defenders of Los Angeles shooting at? As much as this case has been ignored, suppressed and downplayed, it continues to remain an incredible enigma.

Military UFO Battles in the Antarctic—Operation Highjump

On December 2nd of 1946, Rear Admiral Richard Byrd of the U.S. Navy was commanding some 4,000 British, American and Australian soldiers in an expedition to the Antarctic called Operation Highjump. This was the Allies' biggest show of force since the end of World War II the previous year. But given that the war was over and the South Pole was completely uninhabited and inhospitable, what was the purpose of this costly demonstration of military might? On the official level, the mission had six stated objectives, which were:

1. *Training personnel and testing equipment in frigid conditions;*
2. *Consolidating and extending the United States' sovereignty over the largest practicable area of the Antarctic continent;*
3. *Determining the feasibility of establishing, maintaining, and utilizing bases in the Antarctic and investigating possible base sites;*

4. *Developing techniques for establishing, maintaining, and utilizing air bases on ice, with particular attention to later applicability of such techniques to operations in interior Greenland, where conditions are comparable to those in the Antarctic;*
5. *Amplifying existing stores of knowledge of electromagnetic, geological, geographic, hydrographic, and meteorological propagation conditions in the area;*
6. *Supplementary objectives of the Nanook expedition (a smaller equivalent conducted off eastern Greenland).*

But were any of these reasons really worth risking the lives and limbs of 4,000 trained soldiers in the perilous cold of Antarctica? With much of America's military might still deployed in Europe and already stretched too thin in other areas, why would the U.S. military decide to undertake such a hazardous endeavor? Well, according to conspiracy theorists, this was no peacetime research expedition—it was an all-out invasion force sent to eradicate a contingent of Nazis who had fled Europe for a secret Antarctic base called Neuschwabenland.

Strange as it may sound, this story actually does have a kernel of truth in it. The Germans did indeed establish a base in Antarctica back in 1938, and it was in fact named Neuschwabenland. But according to official reports, it was nothing more than a small research station, not a major military base. And even though a number of top Nazis did indeed flee to the Southern Hemisphere after the war, their choice of refuge was generally Argentina, not Antarctica.

But if the conspiracy theorists are to be believed, Neuschwabenland was no mere weather research station near the South Pole—it was the beginning of a vibrant breakaway civilization nestled in the Antarctic. The idea that the Nazis had reverse engineered UFOs crisscrosses into this theory as well, because it is said that both the recovered UFO parts and the new hardware the Nazis created based upon ET tech were loaded into Kriegsmarine U-boats and taken to this base. Supposedly, Operation Highjump was aimed at stopping this ongoing research, and the final battle against the Third Reich took place not in Berlin but in Antarctica.

Okay, so if this story is true, then how did it turn out? According to those who allegedly witnessed it, the U.S. assault on Neuschwabenland was an utter failure. Insiders claim that the mission was ultimately aborted after eight weeks and "many fatalities".

The leader of the mission, Admiral Byrd, also came back from the Antarctic making some rather strange remarks. At one point he even told the Chilean press that they had faced a "new enemy" which "could fly from pole to pole at incredible speeds". However, Byrd grew oddly silent shortly afterward—and in fact he would never discuss the mission again for the rest of his life.

Military Intervention in the Roswell Crash?

Roswell is no doubt the most infamous account in all of UFO lore, and it involves just about every facet of the phenomenon. And one of the major facets of the Roswell incident is the involvement of the U.S. military. So, in the words of former President Barack Obama during a blistering harangue at future President Donald Trump at the White House Correspondents' Dinner in 2011, "What really happened in Roswell?"

Well, there could prove to be an insurmountable gulf between what really happened and what people *think* happened. First, let me give you the basic synopsis of what UFO true believers say:

The Roswell Incident took place in early July of 1947 when a group of extraterrestrials were drawn to the desert sands of New Mexico by the atomic testing activities of the U.S. Army Air Force's 509th Bomb Group. These ETs came to grief when their craft was either struck by lightning or had its navigational systems disrupted by the powerful radar antennas at Roswell Army Air Field. The crewed section of the craft crashed in an isolated stretch of desert, killing all but one of the ETs aboard, while another unmanned (unaliened?) section crashed several miles away on a ranch belonging to one Mac Brazel and left debris strewn over a large portion of his land.

Eyewitnesses later recounted that they accidentally stumbled upon the scene just as uniformed troops rolled up in trucks and jeeps and began cordoning off the area. The military quickly took control, ordering onlookers to leave and even threatening their lives if they dared mention anything that they had seen.

A leading investigator of the Roswell crash, filmmaker and UFO researcher Jaime Shandera, claims to have confirmation of these events through the so-called "MJ-12" documents. The MJ-12 documents were found on a roll of microfilm that was mysteriously left on the doorstep of ufologist Stanton T. Friedman in the early 1980s. They supposedly lay out in detail what happened after the U.S. military retrieved the aliens and their craft.

There are three schools of thought within the UFO community about the authenticity of the MJ-12 documents. Some believe that the microfilm is a legitimate leak of factual information; some think that it is nothing more than a clever hoax; and some say that it is a combination of both, crafted by U.S. military intelligence as a form of disinformation containing some kernels of truth but just as many lies in order to throw UFO researchers off the scent of what *really* happened.

So you'll have to make up your own mind about MJ-12, and to help you do that, let's delve into exactly what the documents say. They read as a briefing put together in November of 1952 for the benefit of then President-elect Dwight D. Eisenhower. The authors present themselves as a "Top Secret Research and Development" group answerable "only to the President of the United States". After describing the background of this group and its 12 members—all high-ranking officials—the briefing slowly begins to introduce the UFO phenomenon. At first it treads lightly, discussing the UFO wave of 1947 and acknowledging that after widespread sightings of unknown craft, the military conducted an investigation to determine just what was invading U.S. airspace. It details how fighters were scrambled on a number of occasions to try to chase down the UFOs, but states that the elusive objects always evaded pursuit. According to the document, the U.S. military was at a complete standstill when it came to understanding what the strange craft were and what they were trying to do.

But the narrative goes on to state that all that changed when one of the UFOs crashed in a remote region of New Mexico near Roswell in 1947. The report claims that on July 7th, routine aerial reconnaissance of the area found "four small human-like beings" some two miles from the main wreckage. They had apparently ejected from the vehicle moments before it crashed, but it hadn't saved their lives. They appeared to have been dead for a while, having succumbed to the harsh desert climate. Their bodies were quickly scooped up by a team of scientists, and the wreckage was hauled away as well.

After the debris were safely cleared away, the news media was fed the story that a "misguided weather research balloon" had crashed in the area. According to MJ-12, however, further investigation had already determined that the wreckage was actually from a "short range reconnaissance craft" most likely sent by some larger mother ship orbiting the planet. Preliminary examination of the occupants also made it clear that they were extraterrestrial in origin, and government scientists gave them the official title of "EBE" or "Extraterrestrial Biological Entities".

The briefing concludes by stating that while the visitors' intentions are "completely unknown", the notable increase in "surveillance" by these otherworldly vehicles should be cause for concern. It also stresses that Roswell and all other ET incidents must be kept secret in order to prevent a "public panic". Addressing incoming President Eisenhower directly, it advises that the "strictest security precautions should continue without interruption into the new administration".

As you can imagine, for the true UFO believers out there, the MJ-12 documents are pretty clear-cut evidence of extraterrestrial contact. Skeptics consider it much more likely that the documents were forged or at least doctored. But if that's the case, it is intriguing how well the forger understood secret military protocols and was able to provide such early insight into what would become the most legendary UFO event of all time.

UFO Chases and Dogfights

A week after ringing in the New Year of 1948, Captain Thomas Mantell was leading a squadron of P-51 Mustangs through the blue skies of Kentucky. They were halfway through their simple training mission when ground control alerted Mantell to a strange object in the vicinity and asked him to take a look. Mantell swiftly located the UFO and gave chase. One member of the squadron ran low on fuel and had to return to base, but the remaining three fighters were able to close with the craft until they were directly underneath it. Mantell began to spiral higher and higher in order to get a closer look, telling his men that he would climb to about 25,000 feet but then "break off the pursuit" if he was still unable to get near the object.

He must have been a little too engaged in his pursuit of the strange metallic craft, though, because as climbed up through the clouds, soaring to higher and higher altitudes, he allowed his air supply to dwindle to such an extent that he actually passed out. He was now in a nightmare situation: His plane was climbing higher and higher, and he was essentially asleep at the wheel. Eventually the plane stalled and began a deadly dive back down to the ground. It's unclear if Mantell regained consciousness and tried to pull up, but after the Mustang dropped back to around 19,000 feet turbulence caused it break apart in midair.

But just what was Mantell chasing? What was the official verdict of the U.S. military in this case? Believe it or not, they said that Mantell was chasing nothing more than the planet Venus! The idea that this seasoned pilot lost his life engaged in the pointless pursuit of a well-known celestial body is beyond insulting.

Just a few months after the Mantell incident, a North Dakota Air National Guard pilot flying over Fargo had a similar close encounter with an unidentified craft. George F. Gorman was lucky enough to survive the meeting—even though he dared to engage the UFO in what amounted to a dogfight. Upon seeing the intruder, Gorman informed ground control that he was going to try to take the object down. But although his P-51 Mustang had a top speed of some 400 miles per hour, it was still no match for this otherworldly vehicle. He soon realized that the UFO was just "too fast for him to catch". But as the object zigzagged and danced before him, Gorman was essentially able to outsmart whoever (or whatever) was piloting it by executing several sharp right turns that put him right in the path of the swiftly moving craft.

Gorman was around 5,000 feet above the ground when the object flew right over him, and although he didn't open fire as he had planned, he got a detailed close-up view of what looked like a brilliant "ball of light". After soaring past, the object disappeared from view for a moment—but then suddenly reappeared on what seemed to be a collision course with Gorman's Mustang. At the last minute, though, it veered off and shot up into the sky above Gorman, almost as if it was showing off. Gorman attempted to follow, but at 14,000 feet his plane began to stall. This was the same thing that had killed Mantell, but fortunately for Gorman it happened at a lower altitude. He still had plenty of oxygen and was still conscious, so he was able to get out of it alive. After regaining control of his plane, he tried to reengage the unidentified craft, but he was unable to get any closer to it and it soon disappeared from sight.

One of the strangest showdowns the U.S. military had with a UFO allegedly occurred in 1951 during the Korean War. According to Private First Class Francis P. Wall, he and his comrades were carrying out an attack on enemy positions some 60 miles south of Seoul when an object like a floating "jack-o-lantern" suddenly dropped down from the sky and hung right in front of them. The dumbfounded troops had no idea what they were looking at, but they assumed that it was some sort of secret weapon deployed by the Chinese, Russians, or North Koreans. They let loose on it with their artillery, but the rounds had no effect whatsoever. Then they tried armor piercing bullets, which they could clearly hear striking the craft with loud "metallic dings"—but which once again caused no evident damage.

After a moment, the UFO started swaying back and forth and its lights began to pulsate with a "brilliant blue-green light". After this ominous prelude, it attacked. According to Wall, the U.N. troops were "swept by some form of a ray that was emitted in pulses, in waves that you could visually see only when it was aiming directly at you. That is to say, like a searchlight sweeps around and the segments of light—you would see it coming at you." Under this ray the men felt an intense heat, and frightened for their lives, they leapt behind the shelter of their fortifications. The craft then shot off across the horizon.

It was later revealed that these soldiers had all been exposed to intense radiation, a fact that would haunt them for the rest of their lives, both psychologically and physically through a steady stream of medical problems. It remains unclear, however, if the ray was actually a weapon or simply some sort of scan to examine the physical condition of the human soldiers. If the UFO was crewed by a group of ET researchers about the nature of

33

human warfare, after all, they probably would have been trying to gather as much data as possible.

Either way, this was one military encounter with a UFO that this particular platoon of American soldiers would never be able to forget.

The Grenada Treaty—Did the Military Make a Deal with ET?

The idea that the U.S. military would secretly cut a deal with a visiting extraterrestrial civilization is an intriguing concept. Even if there is no truth in it, it provides us with a great thought experiment. What would the U.S. military really do if it made contact with ET? If they learned anything from the reaction to Orson Welles' *War of the Worlds* broadcast, preventing panic would be one of their major objectives. But would they go so far as to keep their own citizens completely in the dark about such a monumental discovery?

Some say yes—and they also say that President Eisenhower, who was allegedly briefed about the alien presence in the MJ-12 memo before taking office, went on to sign a formal deal with the ETs known as the "Grenada Treaty".

This supposedly occurred in February of 1954 when Eisenhower was away under the official (and incredibly mundane) cover story that he was going to the dentist. The President was on vacation in Palm Springs when he suddenly dropped out of sight. Speculation about his whereabouts was rampant until it was reported that he had been forced to make an emergency trip to the dentist after breaking a crown while eating a piece of chicken. It was a prosaic enough explanation, but conspiracy theory associated with it is absolutely extraordinary. Because some say that while the world thought he was under anesthesia at some dentist's office, Ike was actually at a military base secretly meeting with aliens and signing the Grenada Treaty.

After all the close calls, run-ins and dogfights with UFOs in recent years, this was supposedly a peace deal—if not a negotiated surrender on the part of the President of the United States. Under this treaty, the ETs pledged to not interfere (at least overtly) with the affairs of humanity, and Eisenhower pledged in return that the U.S. would not interfere with the aliens' business either.

So far, so good—but the ETs also agreed to help the U.S. military perfect certain advanced technologies in exchange for the right to periodically abduct humans for "medical examination and monitoring". The Americans agreed to this on the condition that no humans would be harmed and that they would have all memories of the event erased (a phenomenon that alien abductees would later dub "missing time"). However, the aliens allegedly later broke this part of the treaty by abducting more people than agreed—and failing to return some of them.

Another part of the agreement allowed the aliens to construct—with the aid of the U.S. military—underground bases beneath the remote Four Corners area where Utah, New Mexico, Colorado and Arizona meet. For purposes of inter-species collaboration, the treaty also established a joint base in Nevada that would later be called Area 51.

The most important point of the Grenada Treaty, however, was that the ET presence would be kept secret from the general public at all costs. This was actually something that both sides greatly desired, albeit for completely different reasons.

The U.S. military wanted to hide the truth in order to prevent not only panic but downright outrage. After all, how could they possibly tell their fellow Americans that they had been sold out by their own government? That the extraterrestrials were now officially authorized to monitor and experiment on them? The end result of such a disclosure could only be riots in the streets and perhaps an outright revolution to overthrow the government that had signed the Grenada Treaty.

The ETs, on the other hand, desired secrecy because it was more conducive for their research. If people knew that they were being preyed upon, they might try to interfere with or resist the ETs' experiments. No matter how advanced these aliens were, it was a much easier prospect to abduct humans who were completely unaware of their presence than to attempt to kidnap people who were cognizant of the threat they posed.

Interestingly, the last clause of the agreement stipulated that the ETs would make no other treaty "with any other Earth nation". Some conspiracy theorists say that this explains why the U.S. has had far more reports of alien abduction than other countries—it is the U.S. and the U.S. alone that has agreed to the abduction of its citizens.

Along with President Eisenhower, several top military leaders, notable scientists, and leading community and religious figures were supposedly present at the signing ceremony. Afterward, the aliens apparently returned to their craft and simply took off, leaving the bewildered group of dignitaries behind.

One of the first mentions of this wild tale came a couple of months later in a note dated April 16, 1954. This letter was written by a California writer named Gerald Light to a certain Meade Layne, who was the director of Borderland Sciences Research Associates. Light was a notable member of his local community, as well as a kind of guru for metaphysical research, but not much else is known about him. His letter, however, certainly seems to indicate that something extraordinary took place while Eisenhower was in Palm Springs. Here it is in its entirety:

My dear friends, I have just returned from Muroc (Edwards Air Force Base). The report is true—devastatingly true! I made the journey in company with Franklin Allen of the Hearst papers and Edwin Nourse of Brookings Institute and Bishop Macintyre of LA. When we were allowed to enter the restricted section, I had the distinct feeling that the world had come to an end with fantastic realism. For I have never seen so many human beings in a state of complete collapse and confusion, as they realized that their own world had indeed ended with such finality as to beggar description. The reality of the 'other plane' aeroforms is now and forever removed from the realms of speculation and made a rather painful part of the consciousness of every responsible scientific and political group. During my two days' visit I saw five separate and distinct types of aircraft being studied and handled by our Air Force officials—with the assistance and permission of the Etherians! I have no words to express my reactions. It has finally happened. It is now a matter of history. President Eisenhower, as you may already know, was spirited over to Muroc one night during his visit to Palm Springs recently. And it is my conviction that he will ignore the terrific conflict between the various 'authorities' and go directly to the people via radio and television—if the impasse continues much longer. From what I could gather, an official statement to the country is being prepared for delivery about the middle of May.

According to the letter, Light believed that the existence of the "Etherians" would soon be publicly disseminated. He apparently had no conception of the tremendous lid of secrecy that would be clamped down over the whole UFO phenomenon by the U.S. military—but this so-called "truth embargo" was all part of the agreement made between Eisenhower and the ETs.

Military Intervention at Kecksburg?

Sometime after four o'clock in the afternoon of December 9, 1965, the Eastern Seaboard of North America was lit up by a flash of light that streaked from Eastern Canada to Michigan, to Ohio, and then made a sharp turn and headed off to Pennsylvania. For those who would like to think that what came to be known as the Kecksburg object was nothing more than a meteor, this sharp, controlled turn presents a major problem.

At precisely 4:47 PM, the object slammed into the woods near a town called Kecksburg. Hundreds of people across the Northeast called the police about the light they had seen in the sky, and many Kecksburg residents reported seeing debris on the ground.

At 6:30 PM, John Murphy, the news director at a local radio station, received a call from a woman named Frances Kalp who said that she had been to the crash site and seen a strange illuminated craft partially submerged in the middle of the woods. Murphy contacted the Pennsylvania State Police to see if they could send someone to the site. Believing that there had been a plane crash and that the victims would need help, the police got a hold of Kalp, who agreed to lead them to the crash site. When they arrived, volunteer firefighters were already on the scene looking for the wreckage.

At first, you see, this was very much a community-based response of concerned citizens. Murphy interviewed a number of them, including a little boy who described the object as resembling a "star on fire". In fact, many of the anecdotal accounts we have of this crash come to us from this short interval in which the local residents were allowed to freely express their descriptions of what had just come down in their proverbial backyard.

But this brief window of free speech in regard to the incident was soon slammed shut when truckload after truckload of military personnel converged on the scene. No one was sure who had alerted them—or perhaps they had been following the object on radar the whole time—but they quickly took over all operations at the crash site. Armed men cordoned off the area and ordered everyone to disperse and go home on pain of death.

A few brave souls tried to sneak through the trees to view the wreckage, but they were quickly rounded up and sent packing by the army. Some of the more rebellious even had guns jammed into their face to convince them that when it came to keeping the Kecksburg incident secret, the U.S. military was not messing around.

Still, some who stayed at the edge of the forest managed to witness something that would later become a tremendously important part of the conspiracy theories surrounding the Kecksburg incident. They saw a large military flatbed tractor trailer truck driving out of the forest with an acorn-shaped object, covered with a tarpaulin, on its back. This was obviously the object that had crashed, and all things considered, this was a classic military retrieval operation for a downed craft. The only real question was, what kind of downed craft?

The military's official story was that the object was just a meteor and the local excitement was "not justified". But those who knew about the object's sudden change in trajectory as it tore through the sky—and those who had seen something that looked very little like a meteor being carted away on the back of a truck—had their doubts. Many were even insulted. This was their community the craft had crashed in, after all, so why were they being lied to? It was like the U.S. military had become some kind of occupying force. And all in the name of secrecy? Just what were they trying to hide?

Some thought that it might be a satellite, either Russian or American. The Russian spacecraft Kosmos 96 is known to have crashed on this very day, after all. During the Cold War almost everything to do with spaceflight was classified, so while the capture of a Russian spy satellite would have clamped the lid of concealment down especially tight, for a long time it seemed equally possible that the Kecksburg object was an American prototype of a reentry vehicle for future astronauts.

Then, on the 40th anniversary of the Kecksburg crash in 2005, NASA gave a surprising—and oddly timed—boost to the Russian spy satellite theory with the announcement that fragments of debris recovered in the region had been confirmed to be from a Russian satellite. Suspiciously (to conspiracy theorists, anyway), NASA also admitted that these fragments had somehow been lost at some point in the 1990s. It seemed rather strange that NASA would make such an announcement without the evidence to back it up, and many in the UFO community began to cry foul.

Leslie Kean, a UFO researcher and journalist, actually took NASA to court, filing a lawsuit under the Freedom of Information Act to demand that NASA find and hand over the evidence that they claimed to have lost. So it was by court decree on October 26, 2007, that NASA finally acquiesced and began to search for the lost proof of the Kecksburg craft's origins. But these efforts ultimately turned up nothing, leaving NASA still unable to back up their claims.

The most astonishing claim about the Kecksburg UFO, however, is that it was none other than the Nazi Bell—*Die Glocke* mentioned earlier in this book. As crazy as it sounds, there are those who believe that the Nazis' attempts at tearing the fabric of space and time were successful and they actually launched themselves 20 years into the future from 1945 to 1965! The eyewitness descriptions of the acorn-shaped craft certainly do fit the proportions of *Die Glocke*. But besides this coincidence, is there anything else to suggest that such a thing might even be possible? As good as such a wild tale may sound, the truth is that we will probably never know.

Alleged Armed Conflict in Dulce, New Mexico

As mentioned earlier in this book, a major part of military UFO lore is that the United States made a secret pact with space aliens known as the Grenada Treaty. One of its provisions was that the U.S. military would help the ETs build and maintain underground bases in Arizona and New Mexico.

One of these alleged bases is the infamous Dulce Base said to be situated underneath the desert sands of Dulce, New Mexico. This base is described as a veritable hell on Earth in which ETs run amok experimenting with humans and other life forms on seven different levels of the facility. Each floor serves a different purpose. Some focus on research into exotic forms of propulsion, for example, while others house facilities for biological experimentation.

One of the most jarring accounts about this supposed base relates to an alleged breakdown in cooperation between the U.S. military and the aliens. This breach supposedly occurred in the late 1970s and led to a spate of brief but deadly open warfare between the two groups. The account comes to us primarily from a survivor of the conflict named Philip Schneider, who was a geological engineer contracted to help build part the Dulce Base in 1979. Schneider specialized in building deep underground military bases (DUMBs), which have been in high demand ever since the days of the Cold War.

But Schneider says Dulce was not your typical DUMB. He had to have a special security clearance just to be there, and he began to wonder what he was getting into almost as soon as he arrived, when he sighted several battalions of Special Forces troops standing watch nearby. He knew that if someone felt the need to keep so many of these highly trained soldiers on guard duty here, then there must be something either highly valuable or highly dangerous on site.

And wherever Schneider and his crew dug, the Special Forces were sure to follow. Still, things went smoothly enough at first—and then, while they were digging especially deep one day, they hit a little SNAFU. As the group drilled, they noticed a sulfurous "acrid smell" that quickly filled the whole cavern. Schneider's superiors responded by ordering him into a protective suit and sending him down a hastily improvised elevator. As he was lowered down into the hole that had just opened up in the cavern, Schneider came face to face with a "7-foot-tall, stinky alien"—apparently the source of the bad aroma he had smelled earlier.

Schneider was understandably terrified, but his knee-jerk reaction—reaching for his service revolver and shooting the entity down on the spot—proved to be a bad move. Whatever this creature was, it had friends nearby who heard the gunshot and came running. One of them waved the palm of its hand over its torso, and then a beam of blue light emanated from its chest and struck Schneider, melting off several of his fingers. Not just his hand but his whole body felt like it was on fire as he fell backwards into the elevator and mentally prepared himself to die.

The entities were indeed getting ready to finish him off when a Green Beret hopped down next to him and hit the switch to send the elevator back to safety above. The soldier then jumped out and engaged the beings in a firefight, ultimately giving his life so that Phil Schneider could escape. More troops then converged on the scene, and a pitched battle ensued in which some 60 American soldiers perished. Nevertheless, the Special Forces troops were eventually able to push the aliens back into the subterranean depths.

What were these creatures? What was the U.S. military's relationship with them? And while we're asking questions, did this event ever even happen at all? Well, Phil Schneider stuck to his story until the day he died, which was on January 17, 1996 when he was found strangled by a catheter tube.

It was an odd way to die, but even odder was the fact that it was quickly ruled a suicide. And startlingly enough, shortly before his death, Schneider had begun telling those close to him that if he was ever found dead and it was ruled a suicide—it wasn't. Schneider firmly believed that he was going to be murdered by elements of the U.S. military for being too outspoken about what he had seen at Dulce Base, and that his death would be made to look like a suicide.

So, there you have it. Either Dulce doesn't exist and Phil Schneider was simply a sad, fantasy-prone, attention-seeking individual—or there is indeed a faction of the U.S. military in so deep with ET that they are willing to cut down their fellow Americans—including military veterans like Phil Schneider, no less—in order to keep their dark secrets from the public view. When you come right down to it, it's really a pretty troubling story either way.

The Rendlesham Forest Incident

It was the day after Christmas, 1980, at the Bentwaters and Woodbridge airbases in rural Suffolk County, England. Santa Claus had already returned to the North Pole with his gifts and goodies, but a few American airmen stationed at these British bases still had one incredible treat in store for them.

Bentwaters and Woodbridge were being used by the U.S. Air Force at this time, and the bases served as a kind of "Little America" for their hundreds of personnel, supplying an abundance of all of the amenities they were used to having back home. There were certainly worse postings in the world, and most who were stationed there felt they had it pretty good. Being stationed in England didn't involve much in the way of danger or hardship. There wasn't even a language barrier. Everything was comfortable and routine.

All of that was about to change, however, when Airman First Class John Burroughs saw something so extraordinary that it would stick with him for the rest of his life. What he saw was the

UFO that took center stage during what became known as the Rendlesham Forest Incident. He initially noticed flashing red and blue lights due east from his position and immediately contacted his superior officer, Staff Sergeant Bud Steffens. Steffens took a look and saw the exact same phenomenon: stationary lights flashing in the middle of the forest.

Wondering if the lights might be from a crashed aircraft, Burroughs and Steffens climbed into a car and headed out of the East Gate of Woodbridge and on to Rendlesham Forest to investigate. They entered the forest on a small service road, keeping their eyes peeled for anything unusual. As they drove, they saw a white light emerge in the middle of the red and blue flashes. The light seemed decidedly out of place—and it looked as if it were actually moving toward them. Realizing that they were approaching something more complicated than a downed aircraft, the men turned back to the base to report.

A few phone calls later, Staff Sergeant John Coffey delegated Staff Sergeant James Penniston to go out and investigate. A little past midnight, Penniston joined Burroughs and Steffens and listened to their account of what they had seen. Just as they had done at first, Penniston concluded that a plane must have crashed. But when he voiced this opinion, Steffens shocked him by blurting out, "It didn't crash. It landed."

Penniston and Burroughs then went back into the forest to see what else they could find out. It felt like there was literally something "in the air"—there seemed to be an electrical current running through the very breeze. And whatever this force was, it actually seemed powerful enough to impede their ability to walk at normal speed. They later described the experience as like "wading through deep water". Some have since speculated that the men were experiencing the force field from an alien craft.

The lights, meanwhile, seemed to be exploring the forest, slowly hovering around through the trees. The airmen then reached a small clearing that was being illuminated by an artificial light source. As they stood here, they were suddenly startled by an explosion of "brilliant light". Wondering if they were under some sort of attack, they immediately hit the ground. But after no further aggressive moves were made, Penniston jumped up onto his feet and beheld for the first time the source of all the strange lights they had been seeing.

It was a triangular object floating a few feet from the forest floor, with a "bank of blue lights" on its exterior and a white searchlight situated on its roof. The surface was embossed hieroglyphic characters. At just "3 meters across at the base", the object seemed to be too small for occupants, and Penniston guessed that it might be some kind of remote surveillance vehicle. This suspicion seemed to be confirmed when he glanced over at Burroughs and saw a beam of light shoot down right on top of him. Even as they investigated the craft, someone was obviously watching them back.

A person seeing the same sight today would probably conclude that they were looking at some sort of particularly advanced drone. Back in 1980, though, Penniston had no such point of reference. He had no camera phone, either, so as his jaw dropped in amazement he pulled out his notebook and began to sketch drawings of the craft.

He must have been feeling bold, because the next thing he did was actually reach out and touch the craft. His first impression was how smooth it felt. "The skin of the craft was smooth to touch. Almost like running your hand over glass." But when he touched the hieroglyphic symbols on the surface, the bright white light on top of the UFO rapidly increased its luminosity and Penniston was suddenly struck with an immense sense of fear and dread. Furthermore, the fear didn't seem natural; it was almost as if it was artificially induced by the craft—and this was seemingly confirmed when the fear vanished as soon as he removed his hand from the symbols. Penniston then watched as the craft began to float away. Once it reached the treetops, it suddenly shot off at tremendous speed.

As soon as it was out of sight, the men noticed something strange. There was some discrepancy in their recollection of how much time had passed. For Burroughs it had only been a few seconds since they had come upon the craft in the clearing, but for Penniston it had been several minutes. After comparing notes, they attributed this to the bright light that had been shined on Burroughs. Burroughs himself had no memory of what had happened after he was engulfed in this beam of light, and Penniston recalled that Burroughs had appeared to be frozen or "switched off" during the entire incident. It seemed as if he had somehow been placed in a state of—if not suspended animation—incredibly slowed-down animation.

Two days after the incident, on December 28th, Lieutenant Colonel Charles Halt visited the clearing to investigate. His party found the spot where the craft had touched down, noting triangular imprints on the forest floor. They also used a Geiger counter to check for radiation, and they did indeed find elevated levels of radiation present. But the most famous aspect of their expedition is the audiotape of Halt's real-time comments as they examined the scene.

Soon after they arrived, Halt noticed a bright flashing light to the east. He then saw three "star-like lights" moving above their heads. On the tape, you can clearly hear Halt's startled remarks, and at one point he gives up trying to describe the situation and simply utters, "This is weird!" But as weird as it all was, when all is said and done, we still don't know exactly what these U.S. airmen saw in Rendlesham Forest.

Strange Incursions at Area 51

Sometimes called Dreamland, Area 51 is indeed a hazy dream world where fantasy seems to intersect with reality. The place is so fantastic, in fact, that for most of its history, the U.S military denied its very existence. Although various individuals came forward with testimony of military activity there, until 2013, the Pentagon claimed to know absolutely nothing about it.

So why all the secrecy? The most obvious answer is that top secret military aircraft were being tested at this base. The government didn't want any leaks about these projects, and they decided that leaks from a "nonexistent" airbase would be even less credible than usual. In a Cold War context, such secrecy is certainly understandable, but conspiracy theorists believe there is more to this story than that. They believe that the base hides alien technology as well as top-secret human tech—and also that the U.S. military is working hand in hand with extraterrestrial beings at Area 51.

But before we delve into these theories, let's take a look at the basic history of the base. Whatever else may be true about Area 51, a little bit of factual background will help set the scene.

The land on which Area 51 is located was formerly barren desert inhabited only by a few isolated encampments of Shoshone Indians who had lived in the region for centuries. In 1940, the U.S. military set up a small base called the Las Vegas Bombing and Gunnery Range (the area is around 80 miles north of Las Vegas). After World War II came to a close in 1945, the newly established Atomic Energy Commission requisitioned a sizable portion of the land to carry out atomic tests, resulting in the creation of the Nevada Proving Grounds. Initially the atomic bombs were detonated on the desert surface, but after the Nuclear Test Ban Treaty of 1963, atomic research literally went underground.

The U.S. Air Force, meanwhile, grabbed up another corner of the tract, which had been divided into a grid of numerical quadrants for ease of reference. The portion the Air Force took happened to be labeled Area 51. Soon, several exotic new aircraft were being tested there under conditions of utmost secrecy. These included the U2 spy plane, dating from the early 1950s, and the SR-71 Blackbird, which was created in the 1960s, can soar up to 100,000 feet, and looks like something straight out of a science fiction novel. Eventually, Area 51 produced the stealth fighters and bombers that would capture the world's attention in the 1980s and 1990s. Even more advanced craft are said to be in the works now.

But is all of this the result of military R&D, or is there something else behind it? According to conspiracy theorists, these aircraft are much more the fruit of reverse engineering than human innovation and industry. And not only that—it is also alleged that actual ET engineers are on the ground assisting their human counterparts.

In one of the more fantastical (fantastical even for Dreamland) reports, a man named Bill Uhouse claims to have worked with an alien called J-Rod on flight simulators intended to train U.S. Air

Force pilots in the operation of UFOs. According to Uhouse, the UFOs fly via a direct neural link with the ETs' minds. The entities literally become one with their craft, allowing them to fly by reflex and cutting response time to almost nothing. This is why UFOs are often seen "turning on a dime" and making other incredibly rapid maneuvers. But Uhouse and J-Rod had their work cut out for them; finding a technological bridge that would allow humans to link up in the same way proved to be an extremely difficult proposition.

This strange story was later corroborated by a microbiologist named Dan Bursich, who says he was sent to Area 51 in the 1990s and ordered to "take tissue samples" from live ETs such as J-Rod. The aliens lived in a "perfectly round sphere chamber" that shielded them from human pathogens. Bursich also saw Uhouse's flight simulator, which consisted of a giant "support arm" that held prototype craft in place and allowed "simulated rotation". The craft were powered up by external "energy capacitors". These large batteries could only power the craft for a short time, but it was enough to allow human pilots to try their luck in brief simulated flight maneuvers.

Such training sessions were also documented by the late Colonel Philip Corso, whose book *The Day After Roswell*, written shortly before he passed away, claims that all manner of alien tech is being tested at Area 51. Corso confirmed that the craft were operated by a neural link directly to the ETs brains. The flight simulator could give humans an idea of how to fly the craft, but no major progress could be made until a means of actually linking up a human mind to the craft was created.

Another man who features prominently in UFO lore, research scientist Bob Lazar, claims that he was one of the people assigned to that task. Lazar says he was hired on at Area 51 in late 1988 as part of a team of scientists investigating an "exotic propulsion system". In a classic case of the military keeping things on a need-to-know basis, he was initially told very little about where the new technology originated. In fact, he was simply walked right up to a "flying saucer" and unceremoniously informed that this vehicle would be the object of his efforts.

Lazar recalls being astonished by the strange craft, but he didn't think that it was extraterrestrial in nature. On the contrary, he thought that he had just been given a down-to-earth explanation for "all those UFO sightings". He assumed that since the U.S. military had something like this in their possession, it meant that all the flying saucers being reported in American skies were actually secret military craft.

But when he was allowed into the object, he quickly realized that this simply wasn't the case. First of all, he noticed that the seats, control deck, and other aspects of the vehicle were too small for human use. But even more telling were the alarm bells of his intuition. Lazar couldn't quite explain it, but upon stepping into the vehicle a chill ran down his spine and he just somehow "knew" that this craft didn't belong to this world.

Lazar's worldview may have been mercilessly shattered by this discovery, but he stayed on the project and began work on trying to understand the "gravity amplifiers" which the craft used for propulsion. He also looked into the fuel that these amplifiers ran on, which he claimed was based upon "element 115"—an element that didn't even exist on the periodic table back in the 1980s. It wasn't until 2003 that scientists first synthesized an element with that atomic number, which is now known as Moscovium.

So, what's really going on in Dreamland? Is it home to a military collaboration with ET, or is it simply a high-tech research hub for conventional aircraft? We can only hope that someday the complete and unredacted truth of the matter will finally emerge. Until then, it's all just speculation.

The Pentagon's Partial UFO Disclosure

For several decades now, UFO buffs have been waiting with great anticipation for the day that the Pentagon will finally admit to "what it knows about UFOs". And for just as long, official statements from the U.S. military have consistently denied not only the existence of UFOs but even any military interest in the subject. The Pentagon's official stance was basically that UFOs didn't exist and the military couldn't care less about reports of them.

That changed on December 16, 2017, when the Pentagon finally admitted that it was not only interested in UFOs, but that it had spent over 22 million dollars investigating them in a little something referred to as the Advanced Aerospace Threat Identification Program (AATIP). This program spent five years investigating purported military sightings of highly advanced yet unknown craft—in other words, UFOs—that were threatening the sovereignty of U.S. airspace.

Now, 22 million dollars may seem like a lot of money for a research project, but compared to the Defense Department's 600 billion dollar annual budget, it's just a drop in the bucket. And it turns out that a good chunk of these funds went to a somewhat infamous name in the world of UFO research—Robert Bigelow. This billionaire businessman, the founder of Bigelow Aerospace and the former owner of Skinwalker Ranch, an alleged hotbed of UFO and other anomalous activity, has long been known for his interest in the paranormal.

Allegedly, Bigelow has material recovered from a UFO locked up at one of his facilities. And in this case, it's not the *National Enquirer* doing the alleging—this is a claim straight from the Pentagon. Military intelligence officer Luis Elizondo actually conducted an investigation into the matter and reported that "metal alloys and other materials" associated with an unknown craft were being stored by Bigelow's aerospace company.

This certainly looks like an admission of not only strange sightings but the actual recovery of material. Even so, for five whole years, from 2007 to 2012, this secretive program went largely unnoticed even as AATIP poured everything it had into the investigation of alleged UFO encounters with military personnel. The full report has yet to be released, but what we know as of right now is astonishing.

Seasoned pilots have reported seeing aircraft invading American airspace that are "vastly more advanced" than anything the U.S. military—or even its main rivals, Russia and China—is capable of producing. And when U.S. jets have tried to intercept these objects, they dart around at such mind-blowing speeds that they seem to "defy the laws of physics".

Even more worrying to Pentagon officials was the UFOs' habit of conducting surveillance of nuclear-powered ships at sea and nuclear power plants on land. As previous UFO accounts have related, whoever the ETs are, they seem to be very interested in humanity's development of nuclear technology. Many of the AATIP reports do indeed involve UFO visits to nuclear facilities.

However, one of the strangest sightings reported by the AATIP was of the infamous "Tic Tac" UFO. In 2004, two Navy pilots intercepted an object, described as being "white, oblong, some 40 feet long and perhaps 12 feet thick", encroaching on U.S. airspace in the Pacific. They had just launched from the nuclear-powered aircraft carrier *Nimitz* some 80 miles off the coast of Baja California and were on a routine flight when an air controller from the missile cruiser U.S.S. *Princeton*—which was also in the area—alerted them to an unidentified craft and asked them to intercept it.

The lead pilot (who is listed only as "Source" in the official report but was later revealed to be Commander David Fravor) initially assumed that they would be intercepting a drug smuggler from Mexico. It was quite common for Mexican cartels to use small planes and helicopters to carry their narcotics northward. But then the air controller came back on and asked, "What is your load-out?"—military-speak for "What kind of weapons are you carrying?" Both pilots knew full well that they wouldn't be asked that question if they were merely going after some run-of-the-mill drug runner. Whatever they were looking for, it apparently posed a direct military threat.

Following what she saw on the radar screen, the air controller led the fighter pilots to a particular quadrant of the Pacific before announcing, "You should have a visual!" Initially, neither pilot saw anything, but then Fravor happened to look down and notice that there was a major disturbance taking place in the water below. It appeared to be a circular swath of rough water some "60 feet wide by 80 feet in length". Was this what the controller was seeing on radar? Some kind of UFO invisible to the eye yet capable of disrupting the water below it? At this point, all the pilots knew was that they were witnessing a strange oceanic anomaly. But as they watched this anomaly in the water, a strange Tic-Tac-shaped white UFO suddenly appeared.

According to Fravor's testimony, "The object was opaque with a solid, definable edge. The object did not appear to emit any noticeable light or radiation from its surface, nor did it have any noticeable exhaust trail." Fravor and his wingman watched in amazement as this highly unorthodox vehicle moved back and forth over the oceanic disturbance. It seemed clear that it was somehow involved in unsettling the water below.

They were attempting to follow the craft when it suddenly "reoriented" itself in bizarre "tumbling maneuvers" that had it flipping and flopping rapidly through the air until the previously pursued craft was positioned right behind the F/A-18 fighter jets trying to intercept it! The thing apparently flipped through the air like a rock skipping across a lake. Or as Kenneth Arnold, the famed UFO witness who ignited the flying saucer craze in the first place, described his own sighting in 1947, it moved "like a saucer if you skip it across water". Arnold's description of a bizarre skipping and tumbling motion all those years ago matches up perfectly with what these seasoned Navy pilots saw in 2004. These craft didn't seem to fly through the air as much as they erratically swam through it.

Shortly after this maneuver, the craft shot off again, and at this point the Navy pilots lost sight of it. As they were now low on fuel, they decided to return to their carrier rather than continue the search.

Shortly after they touched down, they were called into a conference room for a debriefing. Word of the strange incident had already spread, and somewhere along the line the commanders of the *Nimitz* had apparently decided to fall back on an age-old reaction to UFO sightings—ridiculing the witness. The pilots walked into the conference room to find the *X-Files* theme music playing and their superior officers wearing tinfoil hats. Whatever the Tic Tac craft may have been, the leadership of the *Nimitz* wasn't taking it seriously.

Flash forward to 2017, though, and the Pentagon was showcasing this report as their best case for an authentic military/UFO encounter. What gives?

Some suggest that the Pentagon is releasing a small amount of its data on the UFO phenomenon as a kind of "trial balloon" to gauge the public's reaction. And when the news was released during the Christmas season of 2017, that reaction was surprisingly muted. The Pentagon was basically admitting that their pilots had been regularly engaging with unknown aircraft far in advance of any vehicles known to man, and while it was never claimed that these craft were flown by extraterrestrials, for anyone who could read between the lines, the suggestion was loud and clear. Yet for many Americans, this long-awaited disclosure seemed to go in one ear and right out the other. There was no *War of the Worlds* panic at the announcement of potential ET visitors—largely, there was indifference. If this was indeed a trial balloon, it went over more like a lead balloon.

But while there wasn't much interest from the public, true believers were predictably enthralled. The 2017 disclosure has reinvigorated the sagging sails of the UFO community by raising the prospect of further disclosures to come. Apparently, the truth is indeed out there—but only time will tell exactly what it is.

What Does It All Mean?
And What Can We Know for Sure?

The topic of UFOs has always been full of mysteries. The obvious mysteries have to do with what they are, where they are from, and what they want. But just as mysterious is the reaction of the United States government—and in particular, the military—in regard to these alleged visitors to our skies.

Because when it comes to UFOs, the official position of the Pentagon has moved around all over the place through the years. All one has to do to see this strange dance at work is to look at the first official studies of the phenomenon sanctioned by the U.S. military. First there was Project Sign, launched after the first major wave of UFO sightings in the late 1940s. Sign took a fairly evenhanded approach, labeling many incidents as truly unexplainable. Someone somewhere didn't like this result, though, so the next UFO study group—with the name that says it all—began as Project Grudge. Project Grudge had a real axe to grind, and from the very beginning it was determined to debunk all UFO sightings at all costs. The study did everything it could to label every single sighting as nothing more than misidentification of common aircraft, the moon, or even swamp gas. Grudge must have been too heavy-handed, however, because Project Blue Book was authorized just two years later. And although it still debunked the majority of the sightings, Blue Book was generous enough to list a small percentage as truly noteworthy and unexplainable events.

After a long period of complete denial, the U.S. military made yet another change in approach in 2017 with the disclosure of its Advanced Aerial Threat Identification Program. Although the word "UFO" is conveniently absent from the discussion, the

AATIP concluded that advanced craft of unearthly origin occasionally *do* appear in U.S. airspace—and that actual materials from these craft have been recovered and preserved.

The 2017 announcement that pieces of UFOs are locked away in storage somewhere came some 70 years after the infamous Roswell crash. The decades-old "truth embargo" the military put in place around UFOs has apparently sprung a leak. Now the question is—will the military top brass turn a new leaf and become completely forthright and transparent over UFO encounters going forward? Or will they just jump ship entirely?

Also by Conrad Bauer

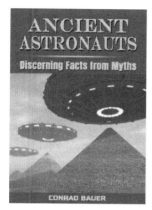

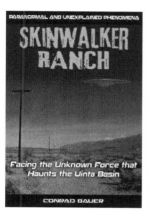

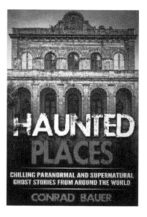

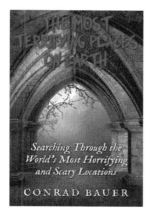
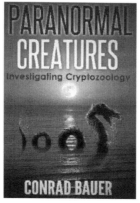

VOL. 2
THE WORLD'S STRANGEST FORGOTTEN CONSPIRACY THEORIES

CONRAD BAUER

The World's Strangest
FORGOTTEN CONSPIRACY THEORIES

CONRAD BAUER

TIME TRAVEL

BREAKING THROUGH THE BARRIER OF TIME

THE TALES OF THOSE WHO HAVE ENTERTAINED VISIONS, VISIONARIES, AND VISITORS FROM THE FUTURE

CONRAD BAUER

TRUE CASES OF DEMON ENCOUNTERS, EVIL ENTITY POSSESSIONS, AND DEMONIC ATTACKS
DEMONIC ENCOUNTERS

CONRAD BAUER

DAMNABLE DEVILS' HISTORY, THEORIES, CONTROVERSIES, AND CONSPIRACIES
DEMONS AND FALLEN ANGELS

CONRAD BAUER

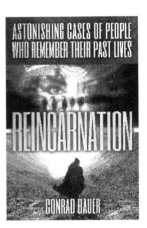

ASTONISHING CASES OF PEOPLE WHO REMEMBER THEIR PAST LIVES
REINCARNATION

CONRAD BAUER

Printed in Great
Britain
by Amazon